Renäe M. Gilley

THE HOUSEKEEPER'S
Cookbook
HEALTHY PASTRY COOKBOOK

THE HOUSEKEEPER'S COOKBOOK
HEALTHY PASTRY COOKBOOK

iUniverse books may be ordered through booksellers or by contacting:

iUniverse
1663 Liberty Drive
Bloomington, IN 47403
www.iuniverse.com
1-800-Authors (1-800-288-4677)

Because of the dynamic nature of the Internet, any web addresses or links contained in this book may have changed since publication and may no longer be valid. The views expressed in this work are solely those of the author and do not necessarily reflect the views of the publisher, and the publisher hereby disclaims any responsibility for them.

Any people depicted in stock imagery provided by Getty Images are models, and such images are being used for illustrative purposes only.
Certain stock imagery © Getty Images.

ISBN: 978-1-5320-6828-7 (sc)
ISBN: 978-1-5320-6829-4 (e)

Library of Congress Control Number: 2019903424

Print information available on the last page.

iUniverse rev. date: 07/25/2019

Contents

Prologue

The Housekeeper's Cookbook

I started this cookbook when I worked with everyone at the diner as a pastry chef. I realized it would help Jen, Jake, and Donna to bake many of the pastries I made after I moved on in my life. Jen is becoming a great pastry chef, and I am very proud of her. I'm still there, working part-time, and I hope by sharing these with you, more people can enjoy the pastries that I have made to enjoy during my life.

Once, I was told that handing down a recipe is sharing a little part of you that can live on in others. I hope as you try these and find some you like, you will pass them on to your loved ones. I can't remember where all of these came from or who gave many of them to me. If there's a particular product that I like better than others, I may list that product, but you can change anything to meet your likes and needs unless I say it has to be that item. A recipe is the ground work for an idea, and you can change it to make it your own.

If you're not sure who the people are that I'm talking about, find the book The Housekeeper that Renae wrote and then you will understand better. I have listed many of these recipes as they were mentioned or made in that book but she may not have pictures for every one of them.

You can pull up almost anything you want to bake on the internet now, and with more than just one recipe for each item. I want to thank all my friends and family that shared so many wonderful recipes with me through the years and for allowing me to share them with others.

To all of you, I hope you have fun as you make and try many of the wonderful items contained in this cookbook. Renae did a great job writing this for me. It was a pleasure to meet her.

Love is what binds people together, and when a person bakes, they love those that will enjoy what they make. I am sharing my cookbook with you so you can share your love.

Rachel

The Housekeeper's Cookbook

By

Renäe M. Gilley

Scones

I have cut this recipe down to make eight at a time so it won't overwhelm anyone. I also prefer to make them low fat for my personal use. If you don't have to worry about your weight, then use the regular items and not the reduced fat items.

2 cups of Bisquick (I prefer the Heart Smart reduced fat)

½ cup Stevia or Trivia or Splenda or Equal (the one that you prefer) or real sugar

½ cup half and half (I use fat-free)

1 tsp flavoring (vanilla is good with any additional items you add, but you can use any extract to match the chips you use, almond, rum, lemon, cherry, orange, peppermint, the possibilities are endless).

Additional items to add to the above dough: I've made many different types of flavored scones.

Chocolate: You can use 1 tsp of instant coffee crystals with ¼ cup cocoa powder, ¼ cup chopped nuts, ½ cup chocolate chips (chocolate milk even adds a lot to this one)

Chocolate chip: ¼ to ½ cup chips, ¼ cup chopped nuts and ¼ cup raisins

Butterscotch: ¼ to ½ cup butterscotch chips, ¼ cup chopped nuts and ¼ cup chopped dried apricots

Cranberry-Almond: ¼ c Dried cranberries, ¼ c sliced almonds, ½ c vanilla chips

One year I found cherry flavor chips: I used ½ cup with dried cherries and nuts

One year I found pumpkin flavor chips: I used 1/3 cup chips and dried white raisins and nuts

You can use anything that you like but try not to add more than one cup total of the extra items.

Mix everything together till a firm ball forms. If it's too moist add a tiny bit more of the Bisquick till you can form the ball. Put it on a cutting board sprinkled with a small amount of Bisquick. Pat it down in a circle until the ball is about ½ inch thick. Cut into 8 equal pieces, like you cut a pie. I use a silicon baking sheet and place the pieces on it, so they don't touch. Bake at 450* for 8 minutes. I can wrap and freeze for my personal Grab and Go breakfast items.

Pie Crust (My mother's)

When I was a little girl, my mother taught me how to make pie crust. Back then, you did not go to the store to buy it; the women made all of their desserts from scratch.

Combine in a large bowl:

  3 cups of All-purpose flour
  1 tsp of salt
  1 ¼ cup of Crisco (that is what my mom used. The new butter flavored Crisco is nicer)

Cut all of this together using a pastry cutter, when ready it should be in small coarse pieces.

In a second bowl combine:

  1 whole egg, beaten
  5 T of water
  1 T vinegar

Pour the liquid mixture over the flour mixture and mix well. If it will not form a ball and is too dry, add a tiny bit of water. If it is too moist add a small amount of flour. It needs to form a ball.

Separate into two same size balls and place in plastic wrap or put in a plastic bag. You will get two pie crusts from this recipe. It's best to refrigerate a couple of hours or overnight before using.

Roll out on a floured counter and lay in your pie pan. Decorate the edges and fill with your favorite ingredients. I prefer to use pancake flour (from a mix) on the counter to roll it out. It is sweet and adds to the flavor when it's baked.

Dutch Apple Pie

You'll need one pie crust, prepared in your pie pan. I prefer to prebake for five minutes, so the pie crust is done in the center when the pie is finished baking.

Apple pie filling for one pie:

8 to 10 apples, peeled, seeds removed & sliced) I prefer red or yellow apples (green may be too sour. I did this once and regretted it.)

> ¾ c sugar
> 1 c flour
> 2-3 T cinnamon

Mix the flour, sugar, and cinnamon together.

Layer the apples and flour/sugar mix in raw pie shell

Topping for the Apple Pie

1 stick of butter

1 c sugar

3/4 c flour

Cut the butter into the dry ingredients and try to put it evenly on the top of the pie.

Bake at 350 for at least one hour and cool before cutting. I say at least one hour because ovens cook differently. You know if your oven is true to time, or if items need to come out 5 minutes early or stay in 5 minutes longer. ☺

Pumpkin Pie

1 unbaked pie shell (but I like to bake mine 5 minutes first)

2 large eggs

1 can (2 cups) cooked pumpkin

1 cup sugar

½ tsp salt

1 tsp cinnamon

½ tsp ginger

¼ tsp cloves

1 2/3 cup (Lg. can) carnation

There is a spice called pumpkin pie spice that contains all 3 of these spices. I used it but like using the three more. If you are going to go buy all three, consider trying that one instead. Use 3 tsp. of the pumpkin pie spice instead of the other three.

Mix all the ingredients and blend well with a mixer. Pour into the pie shell and bake at 425* for 10 minutes. Reduce heat to 325 and bake for one full hour. A knife will come out clean.

Cool and top with whipped cream. You'll get 6-8 slices, of a very nice thick pie.

Custard Fruit Pie

Cherry is my hubby's favorite

This recipe was a favorite of my Aunt. She had a cherry tree in her backyard and would send me out to pick cherries for her to bake a pie. I love to put all different types of fresh fruit in this custard, and the pies all taste different yet wonderful. My favorite is with fresh peaches.

Put one uncooked pie shell in the pie pan you intend to bake in (prebake 5 minutes)

Into that place 8 to10 peeled and sliced peaches (fill the pan half full) (You can use any fruit.)

Over that, pour the following beaten together well:

    6 beaten eggs
    1 cup milk (I use Fat-free half and half)
    1 cup sugar (or substitute for sugar)

Bake at 350 degrees for one hour to one and one-half hours. The edges will be golden brown, and the center should be firm. (Different ovens bake differently so keep an eye on it.) Be sure the center of the pie is done.

You can use fresh cherries for this custard pie, as my Aunt did, just be sure and get all of the seeds (Pitts) out of them.

Banana Nut Muffins

1 ½ cup AP flour

1 ½ tsp Baking powder

¼ tsp Baking soda

¼ tsp cinnamon

1 egg

1 cup sugar

¼ cup oil

½ cup chopped nuts (I prefer pecans)

1 cup very ripe bananas (I freeze mine till I have enough to make this)

Mix all the dry ingredients together and set aside.

Mix egg, bananas, oil, and sugar, beating well. Then fold into the dry flour mixture and stir well using a large spoon. Spoon the batter into lined muffin pans. (I prefer using a medium pastry scoop so they all will have the same amount and bake evenly.)

For blueberry substitute the bananas for blueberries, and maybe omit the nuts. (Toss the blueberries in a little bit of flour before adding to the dough so they will not fall to the bottom of the muffins.

Bake at 350* and check after 25 minutes. It depends on your oven as to how long it will take. Test with a cake tester or long toothpick. It's done when it comes out clean.

Makes around 18.

You can easily freeze them.

Almond Cookie Bars

Preheat oven to 325*

1 ¾ cups AP flour

2 tsp baking powder

¼ tsp salt

½ cup butter

1 ¼ cup sugar

1 large egg

½ tsp almond flavoring (if you don't like this one use what you prefer or vanilla)

½ cup sliced or chopped almonds (but you can use any nut you have)

Sift together the dry ingredients, set aside.

In a large mixing bowl cream butter then add sugar, then the egg and extract, then flour mixture.

Should make around 48

You'll need milk for brushing on the top.

Mix till very well blended. Divide dough into 4 equal parts and form each into a 12″ roll.

Place two rolls on one baking sheet and flatten to 3″ wide. Brush with milk and sprinkle almonds on them. Do not precut.

Bake for 12 minutes, remove from oven but leave on baking sheet 3 minutes. Then cut into 1″ strips. Place the strips on a cooling rack. When totally cool, drizzle with icing.

Icing: 1 cup confectioner sugar

¼ tsp almond flavoring

1 tsp milk

Mix together and drizzle over the cooled cookies. When the icing hardens place in airtight container. You can freeze this cookie.

Cinnamon Sticks

Over fifty years ago, a dear friend shared this recipe with me. I know you will enjoy them.

1 cup sugar

½ cup butter

1 egg, separated

1 cup flour

2 tsp cinnamon

½ cup chopped nuts

In a bowl combine flour and cinnamon and set aside.

Cream the butter and sugar till fluffy. Add just the egg yolk and beat well.

Add the flour mixture. It should be too thick for the mixer, and you might even have to hand knead the dough till combined. It should hold together and form a ball.

Place the ball on an ungreased cookie sheet that has edges, around a 9x14 size and press to the sides. You might even use a rolling pin.

Beat the egg white and brush over the dough.

Sprinkle the nuts over the dough as evenly as you can, press down slightly.

I then like to make a sugar and cinnamon sprinkle mix and sprinkle this over the nuts.

Bake at 275* for around 30 minutes. It will depend on your oven, but 40 minutes would be the longest.

Cut into bars as soon as it comes out of the oven, because the cookies will get crunchy when cool and be hard to cut.

You will get around 42 cookies. (approximately 60 calories each and 3 grams of fat.)

Cinnamon Rolls

There is a very good recipe for home made cinnamon rolls on the packages of yeast. It takes a lot of time, but is worth it. They taste very good.

Quick and Easy Cinnamon Rolls

I'm a big one for finding a quick way to do things when in a hurry. I tried making the rolls using Bisquick, and it turned out good. Make a batch of dough for normal biscuits but use milk and add ½ cup sugar. Make it a bit thicker or dryer than you usually would. Roll out the dough, or pat it out to ½ inch thick. Make the cinnamon sugar mixture and sprinkle it over the dough. I use the imitation spray butter and spray it over the entire rolled out dough then roll it up.

Cut the roll into 12 equal pieces and place on lined cookie sheet. (I like to use baking sheets.) I also sprinkle more cinnamon and sugar over the buns and bake them at 450 for 8 to 9 minutes, just as I bake the scones. Remove and let cool before you icing them. The powdered sugar and milk mixture work fine. They are delicious and can be made in minutes instead of hours. It's not the yeast dough texture or flavor, but they're good.

Chocolate Cringles

½ cup Canola oil

4 -5 oz melted chocolate

2 ½ cups of sugar

4 eggs

2 ½ tsp vanilla

2 cups AP flour

½ tsp salt

2 tsp baking powder

1 cup powdered sugar

Using a mixer, mix chocolate, sugar, and oil. Add the eggs, one at a time, beating well after each addition. Add the vanilla last.

Mix together flour, salt and baking powder then add slowly to the first mixture.

It is best to chill the dough overnight.

Preheat oven to 350. Use a baking sheet if you have one. Using a cookie scoop, put one scoop at a time in the cup of powdered sugar, covering the ball completely. Place the balls two inches apart on the cookie sheets. (Don't press down.)

Bake for 10 to 12 minutes (depends on your oven. Don't overbake.)

This should make around six dozen and is very easy to double or cut in half. I think the original version came from a Better Homes and Gardens cookbook forty years ago.

Pecan-Sandies

My next-door neighbor at my first home taught me how to make this wonderful little cookie. She always made them for New Year's Eve. I thought it was odd, not to bake them for Christmas. She told me they were too special to add to a plate of Christmas cookies and she waited and saved them to be enjoyed separately and not just another Christmas cookie.

I think, if you have never tried homemade ones, you will understand why she felt this way. She said this recipe had been passed down in her family from mother to daughter for over one hundred years. She did not have a daughter, so I was the lucky one she shared it with. I hope you will enjoy it as much as I do. I still make them every New Year's Eve.

1 cup butter (Yes, real butter)

1/2 cup powdered sugar (and you need more to roll the cookies in after they are baked)

1 cup all-purpose flour

2 tsp vanilla (I always use the real thing)

1 ½ cup very finely chopped pecans

Cream the sugar and butter together till creamy. Add the flour and mix then add the vanilla.

This should be firm where you can make balls. If it is not, add a tiny bit more flour till you can work with it.

Take a small cookie scoop and place the balls on an ungreased cookie sheet. They don't rise.

Bake at 325 * for 30 minutes.

Remove the pan and have the next pan ready to go into the oven. Put powdered sugar in a small bowl. Take the warm baked cookies, one at a time, and roll in the powdered sugar then place on a cooling rack.

They are best after they have cooled entirely. Store in an airtight container.

I hate to think how many calories they have or how much fat, but for one day a year, it does not matter to me. It only makes 18-24 cookies.

Peanut Butter Balls AKA Buckeyes

This is a very rich and tasty candy if you like peanut butter. I only make it at Christmas since it is not easy to do. I have found putting a toothpick in the ball to help hold it when you dip in the melted chocolate helps a lot. Honestly this is a ball dipped in melted chocolate.

3 cups confectioner sugar
1 cup creamy peanut butter
½ stick butter melted
1 tsp vanilla
¼ tsp salt

8 ounces of melted chocolate
1 tsp vegetable oil
Melt the chocolate & oil together

Mix all of the above together and form into balls. Place in the refrigerator for at least 30 minutes.

Melt the chocolate and oil for 30 seconds in a microwave. Stir. If not completely melted do it for 30 more seconds. Stick a toothpick in the peanut butter ball. Leave a circle of the PNB showing at the top of the ball. Place the buckeye on parchment paper to dry.

Chill in refrigerator for at least 30 minutes so the chocolate will harden. You can then store in an airtight container for a week or freeze till needed.

Peach Cobbler

Mom said in the olden days, a cobbler was a staple of every household. People would pick fruit and berries from the yard or garden to make them. I have changed it to be a lot easier and conform to a more modern-day style, and a much smaller pan full than I make at the restaurant.

In the bottom of an 8X8 pan melt: ½ stick of butter (you can get by with ¼ stick)

Mix together:

1 cup of flour

1 cup of sugar

1 cup of milk (I prefer fat free half and half)

¼ tsp salt

2 tsp baking powder

After this is mixed together well, pour it into the butter but do not stir them together.

Take one large can sliced peaches and lay them into the batter so that every spoonful will have peaches when you serve it. Then slowly pour the juice from the peach can evenly over the entire pan of dough and peaches. Don't stir.

Sprinkle a tiny amount of sugar (and cinnamon if you want) over the top.

Bake at 350 for 45 minutes. (check after 30 minutes since oven temperatures vary)

I like to serve it with whipped cream or ice cream while warm.

You can use fresh fruit, but you need to cook a mixture of the fruit and sugar water to have the liquid to pour over the top before baking. I find cans of fruit work so much better, and taste better. I have no idea where this originated from, but all the older cooks know about it.

Fruit Cake Cookies (My way)

My father loved fruitcake, but it seems it was a lot of work to make, so mom came up with a way to make cookies instead. She creamed the butter and sugar and made them from scratch. I was in a hurry one day and tried it this way and could not tell the difference. So, here's my cheating way to make an old family favorite, but my mom's recipe is the next one in the book.

1 box of white or yellow cake mix

1 8 oz container of the Christmas fruitcake mix (red and green cherries, pineapple and more)

2 eggs

1/3 cup of oil

½ cup chopped pecans

½ cup raisins (if you like them)

Mix everything together and stir well.

Preheat oven to 350 and place a small pastry scoop full on ungreased cookie sheet

I prefer to use a cookie scoop (like an ice cream server), so all of them are the same size.

Bake 10-12 minutes. Check after 10. They should be brown around the edges and done.

Remove from the oven

Cool in the pan a couple of minutes, then remove and put on a cooling rack. I do not put icing on them but I guess you could. Enjoy.

If you want to make them the scratch way, you can make your favorite sugar cookie recipe and fold in the fruit and nuts, but I will give you my mother's recipe also.

Chocolate Sour Cream Pound Cake

This is my favorite pound cake. I make one every year for my birthday. You cannot use fat-free items, and you have to use butter. It's worth it because it tastes so great.

1 cup (real) butter	¼ tsp baking powder
3 cups sugar	¼ tsp baking soda
6 eggs	½ tsp salt
3 cups cake flour or AP flour (sifted)	4 tsp cocoa (I like to use 6 tsp)
1 cup whole sour cream (not reduced fat)	1 T vanilla (real)

Grease and flour a Bundt pan

Cream butter and sugar; add eggs one at a time;

Mix all the dry ingredients together then add flour mixture one cup at a time alternating with the sour cream in between each cup of flour. At the end add the vanilla.

You can bake this cake in two different ways.

300 * for 1 ½ to 2 hours or

325 * for 1 hour and 20 minutes.

I prefer the 300* which takes longer, but either will work.

Cool this cake entirely before cutting it. It tastes much better after it has cooled. I like to dust the top with powdered sugar in a sprinkle can or use a mesh strainer. I find that this is a very moist cake. After a couple of days, I freeze in slices and take out what I want for that day, so I don't lose it.

Bisquick Pound Cake

I was surprised with how tasty this pound cake was. I had my doubts, but it's moist and the cream cheese flavor comes through. I can make this quickly when I need a fast cake.

1 ½ cups Bisquick (I use reduced fat)

1 cup sugar

1/3 cup flour

3 eggs

4 oz softened cream cheese (I used fat free)

6 T softened butter

1/8 tsp salt

½ tsp vanilla

Preheat oven to 350*. Use an 8x4 bread pan (greased)

Beat butter and cream cheese. Add sugar and beat till fluffy. Add eggs one at a time beating well after each.

Combine all the dry ingredients and add to butter mixture. Beat with the mixer for four minutes. Pour into the prepared ban and bake for 40-45 minutes. Test at 40, then 45 to be safe. Cool 10 minutes then place on cooling rack. Let it total cool. You can dust with powdered sugar or use the icing of your choice. Pound cake is always good without icing.

Pancakes

I have to say that there are so many prepared mixes to use for Pancakes that a from scratch batch is harder than just buying those. From scratch may taste better, here is the recipe that I have used all my life.

2 cups flour

½ cups sugar

1 tsp salt

2 tsp BP

1 tsp BS

2 large or 3 small well-beaten eggs

2 cups buttermilk or sour milk

3-4 T melted butter

Sift together all the dry ingredients.

Combine the beaten eggs, and milk then pour into the bowl of dry ingredients, stir well. Add melted butter and combine.

The batter will remain lumpy, but try and not stir any more than needed.

Prepare a pan with spray oil and drop by ¼ cup amounts onto hot griddle. Turn once when half done then remove onto a dish to enjoy. You will yield around 20 4-inch pancakes. You can make them larger if you prefer.

You can put fruit in the batter in the pan before you turn them (blueberries, sliced strawberries or peaches are good examples.)

Bisquick (my favorite) also has a recipe, and they are delicious and fluffy too. I like to add ½ cup sugar to the batter.

Holiday Crunchy Bar Candy

I found this recipe in a magazine a long time ago, then recently at the gym, a friend brought in a large bagful, sharing with us. I had forgotten how much I enjoyed this. It's both salty and sweet and can be made with many different types of chocolate tops. Here's the basic recipe and I hope you'll experiment and make it your own.

1 ½ sticks butter

¾ cup firmly packed brown sugar

1 tsp vanilla

1 sleeve of saltine crackers

10-12 ounces Chocolate to pour over the finished product

Line a baking sheet that has edges with tin foil. Spray the foil with Pam. Place on the foil saltine crackers (1 sleeve), cover the bottom and make them fit tight, touching as much as possible.

In a saucepan cook: butter (it needs to be real butter. I tried it with margarine, and it's not as good), and firmly packed brown sugar, and 1 tsp vanilla. Bring to a medium boil and cook for 4-5 minutes. Pour evenly and spread over the crackers. (It should be thick)

Put the pan in a preheated oven at 375 *. Bake 5-6 minutes, till mixture is bubbling.

While that is in the oven chop up 10-12 ounces of chocolate or use any flavor chip you want. When the cracker mixture comes out of the oven, sprinkle the chocolate over it evenly. After 5 minutes smooth it evenly. (Don't use kisses, they will not harden back up.)

Some like to sprinkle nuts over the chocolate top, but I do that only if I'm using regular chocolate. When I add a little white chocolate, I don't add anything else. Sprinkles are fun too, especially at holidays.

Cool completely. You can put in the refrigerator to quicken the cooling process, but don't freeze it.

Break into small pieces and store in an airtight container. I know you will enjoy this.

You can use any flavor of chips. I have used pumpkin, butterscotch, cherry, toffee, mint, and the list will go on. Use what you enjoy the most.

PECAN SQUARES

A bar cookie very similar to the Christmas Candy bar.

Here is a super simple but great recipe if you want to try it. It was a friend's recipe.

1 cup butter (not margarine)

1 cup brown sugar

1 cup Chopped pecans

Box of Graham crackers

Line cookie sheet with tin foil. Spray with Pam. Place the whole Graham cracker on the entire cookie sheet.

Boil butter and sugar together for 2-3 minutes, until it begins to thicken.

Add chopped pecans to the butter mixture and pour it over the Graham crackers.

Place in the oven and bake at 350° For 7-10 minutes.

Remove and cool. Then cut or break into half for each Graham cracker or as close to that as possible. The smaller the piece, the easier to eat them. They are so good!

Once I tried putting chocolate over the top and did not like it as much as when I put it on the Christmas Crack. This one is better plain.

Trifle

A trifle is a layered dessert. You can make it using cake, pudding, whipped topping, and fruit. It can be made using ladyfingers, sponge cake, angel food cake, and many different types of cakes or cookies. Make up a bowl of pudding and drain canned fruit or have fresh fruit cleaned, cut up and ready to use.

A sample of one I enjoy is: Use canned peaches, mandarin oranges and pineapple chunks for the fruit drained and mixed together. I use prepared instant vanilla pudding and angel food cake. Start by breaking up the angel food cake, about 1/3 of it, in the bottom of a trifle bowl. Over that layer spread fruit, then pudding then whipped topping. Repeat till all is used and you are putting whipped topping on the top. Cover the bowl and place in the refrigerator. It is better to make it the day you intend to enjoy it, about three to four hours before serving it.

Another excellent one is: Bake a pan of brownies and layer them with strawberries, chocolate pudding and whipped topping. You can throw in a few cherries with the strawberries also. They are delicious together.

You can use cookies, and it will be sweeter. I saw one made out of chocolate chip cookies and strawberries and whipped cream. You can't do anything wrong as long as you layer and use pudding, fruit, whipped topping and a cake base. This would be a great way to use up a dryer cake that no one wanted to eat, (no icing on the cake). The fruit, pudding and whipped cream will soften the cake up.

My Mom's Fudge

1 small can carnation (I use the new fat-free one)

1 2/3 cup sugar

½ tsp salt

½ cup chopped nuts

1 tsp vanilla

1 ½ cup semi-sweet chocolate pieces

2 cups small marshmallows

Combine milk, sugar, and salt in a pan over low heat. Bring to a boil and cook five minutes.

Remove from heat then add the balance of the ingredients. Stir 2 more minutes till marshmallows melt.

Pour into a buttered or lined with tin foil pan. I like 9x9 size best.

Cool and cut into squares. Do not overcook or it will be too hard.

To make vanilla fudge, use white chocolate instead of regular chocolate.

To make peanut butter fudge use peanut butter chips.

Quick Quiche

I saw this recipe on a box of Bisquick and tried it one day, a quick way, and very good.

Mix together:

½ cup Bisquick

2 eggs

½ cup half and half

1 cup grated cheese

1 cup of meat and any vegetable you like.

Salt and pepper to your taste

Mix together and pour into a pie pan sprayed with oil.

Bake at 350* for 35-40 minutes.

Death by Chocolate Cookies

1 (8 squares) package semi-sweet baking chocolate

¾ cup firmly packed brown sugar

¼ cup (1/2 stick) butter

3 eggs

1 tsp vanilla

1 tsp hazelnut flavoring

½ cup AP flour

¼ cup baking powder

1 pack (8 oz) semi-sweet baking chocolate (cr 1 ½ cups semi-sweet chocolate chunks or even chocolate chips)

2 cups walnuts (or the nut you prefer). If you omit the nuts increase flour to ¾ cup.

Preheat oven to 350*

Melt one package of the chocolate in the micro at 30 second increments, for up to two minutes, stir till smooth. Stir in next five ingredients, using a wooden spoon.

Mix flour and BP together, stir then add to the first mixture. Add remaining chopped up chocolate and nuts. Bake for 13-14 minutes depending on the size of the cookie.

A mixer is never used on this cookie.

It will make around 18 to 24 fairly large cookies. I always try to get 24 cookies.

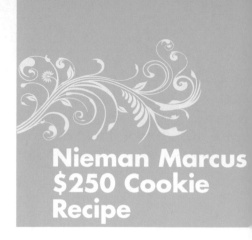

Nieman Marcus $250 Cookie Recipe

This story and recipe have been around for years. My mother gave it to me over 35 years ago. The story goes, two friends were having lunch at Nieman Marcus in New York and were served the most wonderful cookies for dessert. So impressed with the cookie, one of the friends asked if the recipe was available. She was told it could be purchased but the cost was two fifty. She said that was fine and asked they charge it to her account. The next month when she received her statement there was a charge of $250.00 on her account. She called telling them she thought it was a mistake but was informed that the charge was correct. She vowed to get back at them and shared the recipe with the world. Enjoy and pass it on. It makes a very good and rich cookie for $250.00, and the story is good too.

1 cup butter	2 eggs
1 cup sugar	1 tsp vanilla
1 cup brown sugar	½ tsp salt
2 cups flour	1 tsp BP
2 ½ cups uncooked oatmeal	1 tsp BS
12 oz chocolate chips	1 ½ cups chopped nuts
1 8 oz grated Hersey chocolate bars	

Cream butter and 2 sugars together. Adds eggs and vanilla. Mix all the dry ingredients together and add to the butter mixture. Add chocolate and nuts last. Using a small pastry scoop place 2" apart on prepared cookie sheet. Bake 9-10 minutes at 375*. This makes around 6 dozen cookies and the quantity can be cut in half. This would be a perfect cookie for a Christmas Cookie Exchange since it does make so many. It does not require icing because it is so rich with all the chocolate.

Peanut Butter Kisses Cookies

48 Hershey's Kisses, wrapper off

½ cup butter

¾ creamy peanut butter

1/3 cup sugar

1/3 cup brown .sugar

1 ½ AP flour

2 T Milk

1 tsp vanilla

1 tsp baking soda

½ tsp salt

1 egg

Extra sugar to roll cookie balls in

Preheat oven to 375*

Cream butter and PNB. Add sugars and beat till fluffy. Add egg, milk and vanilla, beating well. Stir dry ingredients together and add to mixture. Mix well.

Shape dough into 48 balls. Roll in extra sugar and place 12 to a baking sheet. Bake 8-10 minutes to light brown. Remove from oven and place one kiss in the center of each cookie. Cool on cooling rack. Makes 4 dozen cookies.

Rum Balls (or Bourbon Balls)

In a large mixing bowl place:

3 ¼ cups crushed vanilla wafers (I used the reduced fat ones and the food processor)

1 cup confectioners' sugar

1/3 cup unsweetened cocoa powder

1 ½ cup chopped nuts (any will do and the food processor works great)

4 tablespoons light corn syrup

½ (or a little more if too dry) rum or bourbon (your choice)

Stir all of the above together well.

Using a small pastry scoop, place 1inch balls into a bowl containing additional powdered sugar. Roll and cover with powdered sugar. Place in an airtight container. It's better to let them rest at least a week before eating them. When you open the container, you may find they need to be rolled again in powdered sugar before placing on a serving plate.

If you're not a fan of powdered sugar, you can roll in more of the cocoa powder or dip in melted chocolate, or drizzle chocolate over the top of them. Make them yours. You can even do part in more than one sugar, cocoa or chocolate.

Hot Chocolate Cookie

1 stick butter, soften

¾ cup sugar

¼ tsp salt

¼ and ¾ cup of chocolate chips

1 cup AP flour

Mini marshmallows cut in half

Preheat oven to 350* and line cookie sheet (I use silicone liners or grease it)

Beat butter, flour, and salt till fluffy. Add ¼ cup melted chips to that mixture and beat. Then add the flour, beating well.

I prefer to use a cookie scoop, so all the cookies will be around the same size. Use a small size scoop and drop onto the prepared cookie sheet, 2 inches apart. With a spoon, flatten down into a circle about ½ inch thick. Bake up to 14 minutes. (Not all ovens bake the same. Check after 10 minutes. The longer they bake, the crunchier they will be.)

Remove to wire cooling rack and cool completely.

Melt ¾ cup of chips and spoon into a circle in the center of the cookie (don't icing the entire cookie) then place the cut-up marshmallows into the melted chocolate. Press them down just a little into the hot chocolate icing.

Let the chocolate set up before eating and store in airtight container.

This makes 18 to 24 depending on the size of the scoop.

Very good and great for the winter holidays. Best for dunking into a cup of hot chocolate.

Orange Drop Cookies

1 ½ cup brown sugar

1 cup butter

2 eggs

2 T grated orange rind

1 tsp vanilla

3 cups AP flour

1 tsp baking soda

2 tsp baking powder

1/8 tsp salt

¾ buttermilk (you can make this)

Cream the sugar and butter till fluffy then add eggs. Add dry ingredients alternating with the milk. Add vanilla and orange rind last.

Bake at 350* for 10-12 minutes.

Remove to rack and cool.

Icing:

2 cups powdered sugar

3 T orange juice

¼ tsp grated orange rind

1 drop of red and yellow food coloring (makes orange)

Icing the cookies. It will harden up. You can always use sprinkles.

Molasses Sugar Cookies

1 stick butter

½ cup granulated sugar

1/3 cup brown sugar

1/3 cup molasses

1 egg, beaten

2 cups all-purpose flour

2 tsp baking soda

1 ½ tsp cinnamon

1 tsp ginger

½ tsp cloves

½ tsp salt

You will need raw sugar to roll the cookie ball in

Preheat to 375* Prepare 2 cookie sheets. I prefer liners.

Melt butter in large saucepan. Ad brown sugar and regular sugar, stir to combine. Remove from heat. Add molasses and egg. Combine all dry ingredients and add to butter mixture.

Put raw sugar in a bowl. Using a small pastry scoop, put one scoop in the raw sugar and place 2" apart on baking sheet. If two trays will fit on one shelf in your oven, it's okay to bake both at the same time. Bake 10-12 minutes. They are ready when cracked and puffed, brown around the edges. Put on cooling racks.

Chocolate Chip Cookies

2 sticks soft butter

1 cup granulated sugar

¾ cup packed brown sugar

1 tsp vanilla

2 eggs, beaten

2 ¼ cup all-purpose flour

1 tsp baking soda

½ tsp salt

1 package chocolate chips (you really can use any flavor chip you want)

1 cup chopped nuts (what you like or have)

Preheat oven to 375*

Cream butter with both sugars. Add vanilla then eggs. Combine dry ingredients and add to butter mixture.

Use a small cookie scoop and place cookies on ungreased cookie sheet. It flattens as it bakes.

Bake 8-10 minutes (ovens vary) Check after 8 minutes.

Cool on a cooling rack.

Makes about 60 cookies.

You can add oatmeal to this cookie. Use 2 cups flour and add ½ cup dry oats.

You can use different flavor chips also.

Cream Cheese Cookies AKA Snow Puffs

1 stick butter

4 oz of cream cheese

1 ½ cup sugar

1 egg

1 tsp vanilla

1 tsp almond extract

½ tsp baking powder

1 ¾ cup cake flour

Cream together butter and cream cheese. Add sugar and beat for one minute. Add egg and beat one minute more. Add vanilla and almond extract. Mix well. Add baking powder then the flour in three parts, beating after each.

Place the dough in the refrigerator for an hour.

Preheat oven to 375*. Line baking sheet with a silicone baking sheet.

Remove dough and roll into 24 balls around 1-2 inches in size. Place on baking sheet and flatten slightly, so that they are no longer balls. Too flat and they will not puff up while baking.

Bake for 10 to 11 minutes, till just golden around the edges. Observe them carefully.

Remove to a cooling rack and sprinkle with powdered sugar or drizzle icing over them.

Store in airtight container.

Chocolate Lasagna

I have no idea where I found this, but I remember how good it was. It makes a 9x13 size, so I don't make it often for home. I hope you will like it.

1 package of regular Oreo cookies

6 T melted butter

1-8 oz pkg cream cheese (I use fat-free)

½ c sugar

2 T cold milk

1-12 oz container of cool whip (you can use more) divided in the recipe

2-3.9 oz pkg of instant chocolate pudding

3 ¼ cups cold milk

1 ½ c mini chocolate chips (it's to sprinkle on the top, any grated chocolate would work)

First layer: Crush the Oreos in a food processor and put in a bowl. Add the melted butter, stir till moistened. Pat this on the bottom of your 9x13 pan (I spray that pan with Pam first.)

Second layer: Beat cream cheese till fluffy. Add sugar and 2 T milk and beat till smooth. Fold in 1 ½ cups of the cool whip (any brand will work). Spread over the Oreos and put in the fridge.

Third layer: Whip pudding and 3 ¼ cups of cold milk until thick. Pour over the cream cheese layer. Return to the fridge.

Fourth layer: Top with remaining cool whip and sprinkle the chips or chocolate slivers of your choice over the top for decoration.

Let it sit in the fridge for at least 4 hours before serving.

Bread Pudding

This makes a very small dish of bread pudding. About a 1 ½ quart size.

4 slices bread (I prefer to toast mine and cut into small squares. Hawaiian bread is great to use.)

3 ½ cups milk	Whisky Sauce ingredients
1/3 cup sugar	½ cup sugar
4 eggs, separated	¼ cup water
1 T vanilla (I prefer the real vanilla)	½ stick butter
1/8 tsp salt	
½ stick butter	
½ cup (more) sugar	
¼ c raisins (option)	
½ tsp cinnamon (option)	

Spray your pan with Pam. Put the bread in the casserole dish. Soften bread with a small amount of the milk. Beat sugar and egg yolks together, then add remaining milk, cinnamon and mix well. Add vanilla and salt. Pour over the bread. Fold in raisins if you want them in it. (I like a small amount in it.)

Take the butter and cut into small pieces and evenly place over the mixture. (I think you could use less.)

Bake at 300* for 40-50 minutes. (Depends on your oven.)

The egg whites that are left can be beaten into a meringue by adding 2 T sugar for each egg and beating till stiff. Put over the top and return to the oven at 350* till brown.

Whiskey Sauce

Cook these three ingredients till sugar had dissolved. Then add the whiskey, ¼- ½ c whiskey (what you like). Pour over the dish. Let it soak into the pudding then serve. Some put the dish back into the oven for 5 minutes. I prefer not to do that. Try it and see which way you prefer. You don't want it soggy. Cut and serve. Good with ice cream. Put remainder in the refrigerator.

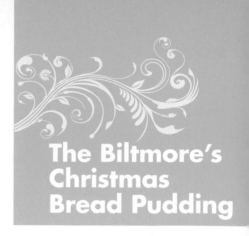

The Biltmore's Christmas Bread Pudding

One year my husband took me to the Biltmore for a weekend vacation. It was like going back in time. While we were there, I commented to our waiter how much I enjoyed the bread pudding and the next thing I knew the pastry chef was walking to our table with a piece of paper in his hand. (Yes, I mentioned to our waiter that I was a pastry chef too.) He said that my compliment meant a lot to him and he wanted to share with me his bred pudding recipe. Now, I am going to share it with you. There are many different ways to make bread pudding, and I bet all will turn out good, but the bread you use has a lot to do with the end results for the flavor. His recipe makes a large pan but you can cut the recipe in half.

Preheat your oven to 350* and you will bake this for around 40 minutes.

8 cups cubed day old bread (buns and rolls work great)

9 beaten eggs	Caramel Sauce
2 ¼ cups milk	1 cup sugar
1 ¾ cups heavy whipping cream	¼ cup water
1 cup sugar	1 T real lemon juice
¾ cup melted butter	1 cup heavy whupping cream
3 tsp vanilla (the real thing)	
1 ½ tsp cinnamon	

Place bread cubes in a greased 9x13 pan. In a large bowl mix all the rest of the ingredients. Pour this over the bread. Bake uncovered for around 40 minutes till a knife comes out of the center clean.

Caramel Sauce

In a saucepan bring the water, sugar and lemon to a boil, and cook till the sugar has dissolved and is a golden amber in color. Stir in the butter and add cream. You can serve it per slice to: You can add the sauce per piece as you serve it, or pour the entire panful over the entire pan of bread pudding. You should get 12-16 servings depending on the size you cut. At the Biltmore he said he gets 12 pieces out of one panful.

I will share with you it was rich, good and enough to share with your date.

No Bake White Chocolate Cookie/Candy

12 oz white chocolate bark

½ cup crunchy peanut butter (if all you have is creamy it will also work. If you do not like PNB omit this item. It will be fine.)

2-3 cups rice Krispy cereal (I use many different types of cereal, use what you like. At times I use one cup of three different types of cereal.)

2 cups mini marsh mellows

1 cup peanuts (or what you like or have)

Where this no bake is concerned, use what you have, want, or like. The white chocolate is going to harden back up and they will taste great.

In a large bowl put the white chocolate and heat in the microwave for 30 seconds at a time, checking till it's melted. Then add the Peanut butter and stir together.

Add to that everything else and stir together.

Place onto parchment paper in the size you want them to be. They will harden up after a couple of hours and are ready to eat. This is one of my favorite no-bake items.

I have made them with semi-sweet regular chocolate but prefer the white chocolate.

Store in an airtight container.

Peanut Butter Cereal Krispy Treats

1 11 oz package of peanut butter chips

¾ cup peanut butter

4 cups cereal (of your choice)

1 cup peanuts

In a sauce pan combine, chips, PNB till melted. Add cereal and nuts and drop by spoonful onto parchment paper. Ready when cool.

Brownie Cookies

2/3 cup softened butter

1 ½ cups packed brown sugar

2 tsp vanilla (I prefer real)

2 eggs

1 ½ cups AP flour

1/3 cup cocoa powder

½ tsp salt

½ tsp baking soda

½ tsp baking powder

1 cup chocolate chips

½ cup chopped nuts (your choice)

Preheat oven to 357* and prepare cookie sheets with silicone liners or parchment paper.

Cream butter and sugar till fluffy. Add vanilla and eggs. Beat well.

Combine all the dry ingredients, mix well. Add in fourths to the first mixture. Fold in the nuts and chips last, stirring till combined well.

Using a small cookie scoop, drop onto cookie sheets. Bake for 9-11 minutes until set in the center of the cookie. Do Not Overbake. They set up more after removed from the oven. Do not cook longer than 11 minutes. Cool on the cookie sheet a few minutes then place on cooling rack.

Dust with powder sugar. You will enjoy this cookie if you like brownies.

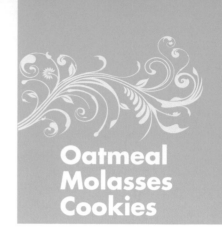

Oatmeal Molasses Cookies

When I was a little girl, I loved it when we went to see my grandmother. She always baked this cookie and stored it in a butter churn with a plate sitting on top. We all knew the cookies were there and that we could have them. I want to share this 100-year-old recipe with you.

Sift together:

1 ½ cups flour

1 cup sugar

1 tsp baking soda

½ tsp salt

1 tsp ginger

¼ tsp cloves

Add to the dry mixture:

½ cup softened butter (or butter flavored Crisco. Back then they used Crisco or lard)

1 egg

¼ cup molasses

¾ cup dry quick oats

Mix with a large spoon till well blended.

Drop by a spoonful onto a cookie sheet. (I use a small cookie scoop)

Bake at 375* for 10 minutes.

Cool on the cookie sheet one minute then remove to a cooling rack.

This makes 3-4 dozen cookies.

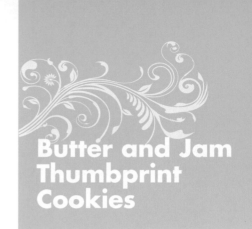

Butter and Jam Thumbprint Cookies

1 ¾ cup AP flour

½ tsp baking powder

½ tsp salt

2/3 cup sugar

¾ cup unsalted butter

1 tsp vanilla

You will need extra sugar
to roll the cookie balls in

Preheat oven to 350*

1 egg

Jam of your choice

Mix the dry ingredients all together. Prepare cookie sheet with silicone mats or parchment paper. Beat sugar and butter till fluffy, about 5 minutes. Add in egg and vanilla till combined, then flour mixture. Combine. Using a small cookie scoop, drop balls into extra sugar, (even colored sugars) then place on the cookie sheet. Put a thumbprint in the center of the cookie and fill with the jam. Keep in mind they do not all have to be the same. Make a couple different ones on each tray. Bake for around 15 minutes, till golden brown around the edges. Makes 24-30 cookies.

Chocolate Covered PNB & Crackers

In a double boiler melt around a pound of chocolate. If it becomes too dry add a small amount of oil. Take two ritz crackers, or two vanilla wafers. Put a small amount of peanut butter between the two, then dip in the melted chocolate. Place on a cooling rack or parchment paper. You can speed the cooling process by placing them in the refrigerator.

Kentucky Pie

You will need one unbaked pie shell

4 eggs

¾ cup sugar

¼ cup brown sugar

1 cup chopped pecans

1 tsp vanilla

1 cup corn syrup

1 stick butter, melted

1 cup chocolate chips (the tiny ones or best)

1 T flour

Melt the butter. Sit aside to cool some. Beat eggs then add the balance of the ingredients to them. Then fold in the butter. Pour into the prepared pie shell and bake at 3508 for 45 minutes. Cut into 8 pieces.

Kentucky Bourbon Cake

After I moved to Kentucky, I found that this cake was a famous one here. Donna taught me how to make it so I want to share this cake with you.

1 pkg of yellow cake mix (I like the butter cake mix best)

1 lg box (3.4 oz) instant vanilla pudding mix

4 eggs	1 cup chopped nuts (pecans)
½ cup oil	½ cup Bourbon
½ cup water	½ cup sugar
½ cup Kentucky Bourbon	
½ c butter (I have used margarine but the butter flavor is better)	

Combine all of the ingredients in the top section then fold in the nuts. Pour into a prepared Bundt pan and bake at 325* for 50-55 minutes.

Heat the balance of the bourbon, butter and sugar in a saucepan till the sugar has dissolved. When you removed the cake from the oven, pour this mixture evenly over the cake. Cool and remove from the cake pan. Cool completely before you slice and serve. You should get around 16 pieces to serve.

Printed in the United States
By Bookmasters